MW01147599

STRONGER
ME

PERSONAL GROWTH JOURNAL

STRONGER ME

Growing in Spiritual
MATURITY & ENGAGEMENT

As a KUEST Student Leader, you are familiar with the

KUEST CODE

1 Timothy 4:12
*Don't let anyone think less of you because you
are young. Be an example to all believers in word,
in conduct, in love, in spirit, in faith, in purity.*

This is the foundation of being a great leader. In the verses that follow, Paul continues to give Timothy specific instruction for how to become this strong leader:

1 Timothy 4:13-16

13 Until I get there, focus on reading the Scriptures to the church, encouraging the believers, and teaching them.

14 Do not neglect the spiritual gift you received through the prophecy spoken over you when the elders of the church laid their hands on you.

15 Give your complete attention to these matters. Throw yourself into your tasks so that everyone will see your progress.

16 Keep a close watch on how you live and on your teaching. Stay true to what is right for the sake of your own salvation and the salvation of those who hear you.

All of these instructions fall into two categories: Becoming more spiritually mature, and becoming more engaged in doing the work of ministry. It is from these scriptures that we receive the goal of becoming stronger in Maturity and Engagement, or STRONGER M.E.

A MORE MATURE AND ENGAGED YOU
IS A STRONGER YOU!

We have designed this journal to specifically help you grow in these two areas. Through daily study of the Word and ideas, through the memorizing of key scriptures and through the discipline of reflecting and writing your thoughts, you will grow. You will become more spiritually mature. You will grow in using your gifts and engaging in the work of ministry. So come on, let's get started, we believe you are ready to become a...

Read the principle and the scriptures below. These are the ideas you want to have strong in your heart. Take your time and think about what you are reading. When you have finished this page, place a checkmark next to DAY 1.

PRINCIPLE

GOD IS OMNIPOTENT; HE IS ALL POWERFUL

God is OMNIPOTENT (OM-NI-PO-TENT). OMNI means "ALL" and POTENT means "POWERFUL". God is ALL POWERFUL. God is able to do anything, He is our ALL POWERFUL God. There is no obstacle, no problem, no enemy that God cannot overcome. Nothing can stop God. He is the creator of everything and our life comes from Him. When we live our lives for God, we are able to tap into His power which helps us to live the good life. We can win against sin, sickness, lack and fear through God's great POWER!

SCRIPTURES
Growing in your knowledge of the Word.

☐ Psalms 68:34 NLT Tell everyone about God's power. His majesty shines down on Israel; his strength is mighty in the heavens.

☐ Ephesians 6:10 NLT A final word: Be strong in the Lord and in his mighty power.

☐ Psalms 147:5 NLT How great is our Lord! His power is absolute! His understanding is beyond comprehension!

Place a check-mark next to the scripture you plan to memorize this week. Once you have recited it to a parent or leader, write the scripture in the appropriate box on your Memorized Word page.

4

○ DAYS 2-4

STRONGER HEART

For the next three days, you will read the lesson below. For each day you will mark the part of the lesson that stands out to you on that day. Each day requires you to use a different method. When you have completed marking the lesson for that day, checkmark the circle.

○ **DAY 2 | <u>Underline</u>**   ○ **DAY 3 | Ⓒircle**   ○ **DAY 4 | [Bracket]**

GOD IS THE SOURCE OF ALL POWER

There are little outlets all over your house into which you can plug anything that needs power. A TV, a vacuum, a video game or anything else that is made to be plugged into power. You might think that the little outlets are the source of power in your house, but that is not completely true. The outlets actually get their power from another source. Somewhere in your town there is a big POWER PLANT that makes power for your entire community. Large pieces of equipment work day and night to create power for every home and business in your town. The outlets in your house simply pass that power to whatever you plug into the outlet. In life, God is like the POWER PLANT and we are like the outlets. He is the source of all power and we are through whom the power flows into our own lives and the lives of others. God's Power helps us make good choices, overcome fear, share hope with others, do well in school, and on and on. He is ALL POWERFUL. Nothing can stop our God. And He has made His power available to us by faith. By believing in and trusting in God, we can have all the wisdom, courage, kindness, patience, peace and healing we need. There is nothing God cannot do, and through faith in God all things are possible for us.

Did you learn more about God's Love or God's Plan? Maybe you learned more about His Character or Truth. Place a checkmark in the box next to what you feel you learned about God. Then take a minute to write what you learned.

○ **GOD'S LOVE**

○ **GOD'S CHARACTER**

○ **GOD'S TRUTH**

○ **GOD'S PLAN**

Finish these final steps for today's journal. Checkmark each completed task.

○ **HOW DO YOU PLAN TO MAKE THIS A PART OF YOUR EVERY DAY LIFE?**
[Write your answer in the appropriate **MY PLAN** Box in the back of this journal]

○ **WHAT IS ONE POTENTIAL AREA OF WEAKNESS YOU WILL ASK THE HOLY SPIRIT TO HELP YOU MAKE STRONGER?**

[Stop now and ask the Holy Spirit for help in this area]

○ **ENCOURAGE A FRIEND**
[Share empowering thoughts, ideas, words, and scriptures with your friends. Know what's going on in your friends lives. Make those things a matter of prayer. Find and share scriptures to encourage them.]

THE NAME OF THE FRIEND YOU ENCOURAGED:

THIS IS WHAT I DID: [circle all that you did]

called them   texted them   emailed them   talked to them   wrote a letter

6

MY PERSONAL
NOTES

Read the principle and the scriptures below. These are the ideas you want to have strong in your heart. Take your time and think about what you are reading. When you have finished this page, place a checkmark next to DAY 1.

PRINCIPLE

GOD IS OMNISCIENT, HE IS ALL KNOWING

God is OMNISCIENT (OM-NI-SHENT). OMNI means "ALL" and SCIENT means "KNOWLEDGE". God is ALL KNOWING. God knows everything. Not just everything there IS to know, but everything there WAS and ever WILL BE to know. God knows the past, present and future. God knows how many hairs are on every person's head, he knows exactly the right choices for us to make, He knows how to help us, He knows how to lead us. He knows what we have done, what we think and why we think it. God knows everything.

SCRIPTURES

Growing in your knowledge of the Word.

☐ Romans 11:33a NLT Oh, how great are God's riches and wisdom and knowledge!...

☐ 1 Samuel 2:3 ESV ...for the Lord is a God of knowledge, and by Him actions are weighed.

☐ 1 John 3:20 ESV Even if we feel guilty, God is greater than our feelings, and he knows everything.

Place a check-mark next to the scripture you plan to memorize this week. Once you have recited it to a parent or leader, write the scripture in the appropriate box on your Memorized Word page.

8

For the next three days, you will read the lesson below. For each day you will mark the part of the lesson that stands out to you on that day. Each day requires you to use a different method. When you have completed marking the lesson for that day, checkmark the circle.

○ **DAY 2 | Underline**   ○ **DAY 3 | Circle**   ○ **DAY 4 | [Bracket]**

GOD KNOWS EVERYTHING!

Imagine that your school teacher told you that your homework was to count the number of blades of grass in your entire yard, the number of ants in the grass, the number of leaves on all the trees and to know all the birds in the trees individually by name...by the end of the week! That would be impossible for us. God not only knows all that for our yard, but for every yard in the whole world. He also knows our heart, our hurts, what we love and why we say the things we say. God even knows what we think. He knows what we really meant when we said that one thing. God is not surprised by anything that goes on in our lives or in the entire Earth. He knows it ALL. He knows when the sun will come up every day, how hot it is burning, just the right temperature to set for the days and just the right amount of rain to keep the Earth in balance. God knows how everything works, after all, He created it. God also knows how to use one of His children to help someone in need in a way that both people are blessed. God knows what you need before you need it and He loves to use His knowledge to help us. There is NOTHING God does not know. So when we love and serve and follow God, He helps us to know what we need to know.

Did you learn more about God's Love or God's Plan? Maybe you learned more about His Character or Truth. Place a checkmark in the box next to what you feel you learned about God. Then take a minute to write what you learned.

○ **GOD'S LOVE**

○ **GOD'S CHARACTER**

○ **GOD'S TRUTH**

○ **GOD'S PLAN**

Finish these final steps for today's journal. Checkmark each completed task.

○ **HOW DO YOU PLAN TO MAKE THIS A PART OF YOUR EVERY DAY LIFE?**

[Write your answer in the appropriate **MY PLAN** Box in the back of this journal]

○ **WHAT IS ONE POTENTIAL AREA OF WEAKNESS YOU WILL ASK THE HOLY SPIRIT TO HELP YOU MAKE STRONGER?**

[Stop now and ask the Holy Spirit for help in this area]

○ **ENCOURAGE A FRIEND**

[Share empowering thoughts, ideas, words, and scriptures with your friends. Know what's going on in your friends lives. Make those things a matter of prayer. Find and share scriptures to encourage them.]

THE NAME OF THE FRIEND YOU ENCOURAGED:

THIS IS WHAT I DID: [circle all that you did]

called them   texted them   emailed them   talked to them   wrote a letter

MY PERSONAL NOTES

WEEK #3
○ DAY 1

Read the principle and the scriptures below. These are the ideas you want to have strong in your heart. Take your time and think about what you are reading. When you have finished this page, place a checkmark next to DAY 1.

PRINCIPLE

GOD IS OMNIPRESENT, HE IS EVERYWHERE

God is OMNIPRESENT (OM-NI-PREZ-ENT). OMNI means "ALL" and PRESENT means "HERE". God is ALL HERE (EVERYWHERE). God is everywhere near every person in every part of our world. He is beyond our world as well. He is present in Heaven, in the Earth and in our heart. There is never a time in your life when God is not near you. He sees and knows everything because He is everywhere all the time. He is with you now, and will be with you in every moment you ever experience. He was, is and always will be.

SCRIPTURES
Growing in your knowledge of the Word.

☐ Revelation 1:8 NLT "I am the Alpha and the Omega—the beginning and the end," says the Lord God. "I am the one who is, who always was, and who is still to come—the Almighty One."

☐ Proverbs 15:3 NLT The LORD is watching everywhere, keeping his eye on both the evil and the good.

☐ Jeremiah 23:24 NLT Can anyone hide from me in a secret place? Am I not everywhere in all the heavens and earth?" says the LORD.

Place a check-mark next to the scripture you plan to memorize this week. Once you have recited it to a parent or leader, write the scripture in the appropriate box on your Memorized Word page.

○ DAYS 2-4

STRONGER HEART

For the next three days, you will read the lesson below. For each day you will mark the part of the lesson that stands out to you on that day. Each day requires you to use a different method. When you have completed marking the lesson for that day, checkmark the circle.

○ DAY 2 | <u>Underline</u>   ○ DAY 3 | (Circle)   ○ DAY 4 | [Bracket]

GOD IS EVERYWHERE ALL THE TIME

How cool would it be to be able to hang out with your best friends, play baseball with your baseball team, attend your tumbling class, go have ice cream with your family, watch your favorite TV show and go to church....ALL AT THE SAME TIME?! God can do that. In fact, God does that. He is present all over the Earth twenty-four-hours-a-day, 7 days a week with everyone. There is not a second of our every day that God is not present with every person on this planet. He sees everything and is never far from us. When we are all alone in the dark, God is there. When we are surrounded by a huge crowd, He is there. When we are just with a few of our family members or friends, He is there. When we are on a high mountain, He is there. When we are in a low, low valley, He is there. When we are hurt, when we are happy, when we are sad, or mad or sick or healthy, He is there. We can always call out to God because God is always there for us. There is never a time in your whole life when God is far from you because God is OMNIPRESENT, He is everywhere all the time. God is in Heaven and He is with you here in this room as you read this journal. You are never far from God because God is everywhere and is near you.

13

www.KUEST.org

WHAT YOU LEARNED ◯ DAY 5

Did you learn more about God's Love or God's Plan? Maybe you learned more about His Character or Truth. Place a checkmark in the box next to what you feel you learned about God. Then take a minute to write what you learned.

◯ **GOD'S LOVE**

◯ **GOD'S CHARACTER**

◯ **GOD'S TRUTH**

◯ **GOD'S PLAN**

Finish these final steps for today's journal. Checkmark each completed task.

◯ **HOW DO YOU PLAN TO MAKE THIS A PART OF YOUR EVERY DAY LIFE?**

[Write your answer in the appropriate **MY PLAN** Box in the back of this journal]

◯ **WHAT IS ONE POTENTIAL AREA OF WEAKNESS YOU WILL ASK THE HOLY SPIRIT TO HELP YOU MAKE STRONGER?**

[Stop now and ask the Holy Spirit for help in this area]

◯ **ENCOURAGE A FRIEND**

[Share empowering thoughts, ideas, words, and scriptures with your friends. Know what's going on in your friends lives. Make those things a matter of prayer. Find and share scriptures to encourage them.]

THE NAME OF THE FRIEND YOU ENCOURAGED:

THIS IS WHAT I DID: [circle all that you did]

called them   texted them   emailed them   talked to them   wrote a letter

14

MY PERSONAL NOTES

Read the principle and the scriptures below. These are the ideas you want to have strong in your heart. Take your time and think about what you are reading. When you have finished this page, place a checkmark next to DAY 1.

PRINCIPLE

GOD IS IMMUTABLE, HE DOES NOT CHANGE

God is IMMUTABLE (EM-MUTE-ABLE). IM means "NOT" and MUTABLE means "Changeable". God is not changeable. In other words, it is impossible for God to change. Nothing that God has ever said will ever change. His promises will always be true. His laws will always remain the same. His truth will never change. God has been the same from before the beginning of time. This is important for us because it means we can always depend on God to always be faithful to His promises for our lives, always and forever.

SCRIPTURES

Growing in your knowledge of the Word.

☐ Malachi 3:6a NLT "I am the LORD, and I do not change..."

☐ Hebrews 13:8 NLT Jesus Christ is the same yesterday, today, and forever.

☐ James 1:17 NLT Whatever is good and perfect comes down to us from God our Father, who created all the lights in the heavens. He never changes or casts a shifting shadow.

Place a check-mark next to the scripture you plan to memorize this week. Once you have recited it to a parent or leader, write the scripture in the appropriate box on your Memorized Word page.

16

STRONGER HEART

For the next three days, you will read the lesson below. For each day you will mark the part of the lesson that stands out to you on that day. Each day requires you to use a different method. When you have completed marking the lesson for that day, checkmark the circle.

○ DAY 2 | <u>Underline</u>   ○ DAY 3 | (Circle)   ○ DAY 4 | [Bracket]

GOD NEVER CHANGES

Everything around us is always changing. In summer, trees have green, healthy leaves. In autumn, their leaves turn brown, orange and yellow and fall to the ground. In the winter, the trees have no leaves. Some days the wind blows, other days it rains, or the sun shines or there is snow and it's cold. Some days you wake up and feel fantastic. Sometimes you might feel tired. You are getting older and smarter every day. Your clothes, the food you eat, it will all change. Everything around us is constantly and always changing. Even though someone takes care of you now, you will grow up, get a job, maybe get married and live on your own. Everything changes in our world. Everything except God. God is always the same. God always loves us. God is always patient with us. When God makes a promise, that promise lasts forever and never changes. God is the same as He was yesterday and He will be the same tomorrow. You don't have to wonder if God will be there for you today, or tomorrow or even next week, because God is always the same. He will always forgive you if you ask, He will help you if you call on Him in faith. Whatever He has ever done for anyone, He will do for you. You can count on God because God never changes.

WHAT YOU LEARNED ○ DAY 5

Did you learn more about God's Love or God's Plan? Maybe you learned more about His Character or Truth. Place a checkmark in the box next to what you feel you learned about God. Then take a minute to write what you learned.

○ **GOD'S LOVE**

○ **GOD'S CHARACTER**

○ **GOD'S TRUTH**

○ **GOD'S PLAN**

Finish these final steps for today's journal. Checkmark each completed task.

● **HOW DO YOU PLAN TO MAKE THIS A PART OF YOUR EVERY DAY LIFE?**
[Write your answer in the appropriate **MY PLAN** Box in the back of this journal]

● **WHAT IS ONE POTENTIAL AREA OF WEAKNESS YOU WILL ASK THE HOLY SPIRIT TO HELP YOU MAKE STRONGER?**

[Stop now and ask the Holy Spirit for help in this area]

● **ENCOURAGE A FRIEND**
[Share empowering thoughts, ideas, words, and scriptures with your friends. Know what's going on in your friends lives. Make those things a matter of prayer. Find and share scriptures to encourage them.]

THE NAME OF THE FRIEND YOU ENCOURAGED:

THIS IS WHAT I DID: [circle all that you did]

called them   texted them   emailed them   talked to them   wrote a letter

18

MY PERSONAL
NOTES

WEEK #5
○ DAY 1

Read the principle and the scriptures below. These are the ideas you want to have strong in your heart. Take your time and think about what you are reading. When you have finished this page, place a checkmark next to DAY 1.

PRINCIPLE
THE NATURE OF GOD IS LOVE

God IS Love. Love is God's nature. In other words, love is natural for God. Love begins in God. Love is who God is. God does not just show love for us, God IS love. We do not learn to love and then learn to love God, God put love in us when He created us. God made Adam and Eve and the Love of God was put in them by the fact that he made them. In fact, when we say God made Adam and Eve we are saying LOVE made Adam and Eve. Love made you, because God made you and God is Love.

SCRIPTURES
Growing in your knowledge of the Word.

☐ John 3:16 NLT "For God loved the world so much that he gave his one and only Son, so that everyone who believes in him will not perish but have eternal life.

☐ Romans 5:5b NLT For we know how dearly God loves us, because he has given us the Holy Spirit to fill our hearts with his love.

☐ 1 John 4:16 NLT We know how much God loves us, and we have put our trust in his love. God is love, and all who live in love live in God, and God lives in them.

Place a check-mark next to the scripture you plan to memorize this week. Once you have recited it to a parent or leader, write the scripture in the appropriate box on your Memorized Word page.

20

STRONGER HEART

For the next three days, you will read the lesson below. For each day you will mark the part of the lesson that stands out to you on that day. Each day requires you to use a different method. When you have completed marking the lesson for that day, checkmark the circle.

◯**DAY 2 | Underline**   ◯**DAY 3 | Circle**   ◯**DAY 4 | [Bracket]**

THE NATURE OF GOD IS LOVE.

The most important fact that you need to remember about God is that at all times, no matter what, He always loves us. God's love for us is bigger and stronger than the power of any wrong we could ever do. And if we will bring the wrong things we have done to God and ask for his forgiveness, His love will always cause Him to forgive us. God does great things for us because He loves us. God made all that there is because He loves us. From the very first day that He created Adam God has loved, and always will love us. The truth is that God does not just love us, God is love for us. Everything about God is based on the fact that God is Love. God does not have to find a reason to love us, God is love and so love just naturally flows from God. His first response to us is love. Sometimes that love causes Him to correct us. When we feel badly about something we have done, that is God, through the Holy Spirit trying to help us learn right from wrong. When we feel compassion toward someone else, that is God, through the Holy Spirit showing us the love that God feels toward them. It is not in God's nature to hate anyone, though He does hate sin. It is not in God's nature to be selfish because Love is always generous and God is Love.

WHAT YOU LEARNED ○ DAY 5

Did you learn more about God's Love or God's Plan? Maybe you learned more about His Character or Truth. Place a checkmark in the box next to what you feel you learned about God. Then take a minute to write what you learned.

○ **GOD'S LOVE**

○ **GOD'S CHARACTER**

○ **GOD'S TRUTH**

○ **GOD'S PLAN**

Finish these final steps for today's journal. Checkmark each completed task.

○ **HOW DO YOU PLAN TO MAKE THIS A PART OF YOUR EVERY DAY LIFE?**
[Write your answer in the appropriate **MY PLAN** Box in the back of this journal]

○ **WHAT IS ONE POTENTIAL AREA OF WEAKNESS YOU WILL ASK THE HOLY SPIRIT TO HELP YOU MAKE STRONGER?**
[Stop now and ask the Holy Spirit for help in this area]

○ **ENCOURAGE A FRIEND**
[Share empowering thoughts, ideas, words, and scriptures with your friends. Know what's going on in your friends lives. Make those things a matter of prayer. Find and share scriptures to encourage them.]

THE NAME OF THE FRIEND YOU ENCOURAGED:

THIS IS WHAT I DID: [circle all that you did]

called them   texted them   emailed them   talked to them   wrote a letter

22

MY PERSONAL
NOTES

WEEK #6
○ DAY 1

Read the principle and the scriptures below. These are the ideas you want to have strong in your heart. Take your time and think about what you are reading. When you have finished this page, place a checkmark next to DAY 1.

PRINCIPLE
THE NATURE OF GOD IS PERFECTION

God IS Perfect. God has never, and will never, make a mistake. His ways, His thoughts, His actions, His ideas, His plans, His wisdom, His timing are always perfect. God never makes a mistake. The world he created is perfect. All of his creatures, including man, are perfect. God sees every possibility and can bring them all together into the perfect combination for every situation. The earth is just the right distance from the sun. The air is just the right combination of gasses for us to breath. That's just the way God works, He is PERFECT.

SCRIPTURES
Growing in your knowledge of the Word.

☐ Psalms 18:30 NLT God's way is perfect. All the LORD's promises prove true. He is a shield for all who look to him for protection.

☐ Matthew 5:48 NLT But you are to be perfect, even as your Father in heaven is perfect.

☐ Deuteronomy 32:4 NLT He is the Rock; his deeds are perfect. Everything he does is just and fair. He is a faithful God who does no wrong; how just and upright he is!

Place a check-mark next to the scripture you plan to memorize this week. Once you have recited it to a parent or leader, write the scripture in the appropriate box on your Memorized Word page.

24

○ DAYS 2-4

STRONGER HEART

For the next three days, you will read the lesson below. For each day you will mark the part of the lesson that stands out to you on that day. Each day requires you to use a different method. When you have completed marking the lesson for that day, checkmark the circle.

○ DAY 2 | <u>Underline</u>   ○ DAY 3 | Circle   ○ DAY 4 | [Bracket]

THE NATURE OF GOD IS <u>PERFECTION</u>.

Imagine taking a pencil and trying to draw a perfect circle on a piece of paper. Every now and then, if you try really hard, you might be able to make a circle that is perfectly round. Now imagine being able to do that every time you ever draw a circle on every piece of paper. In fact, can you imagine never making a mistake ever? That is what it is like to be God. It is PERFECTION. God's plans and ideas for our lives are perfect. They are just the right combination to help us enjoy life, make good things happen and be a blessing to others. In fact, God's plan is so perfect that if everyone followed His plan, life would be exciting, fun and full of good things for everyone all the time. The Bible teaches us that we should do our best to follow God's perfect plan all the time. We should always be looking out for the best interest of others, trying to find ways to be more and more like God and enjoying life. Even though God is perfect, we are not always perfect. We do make mistakes. We don't always get the plan just right. But God still loves us and still has a perfect plan for our lives. And even when we mess up, God is still able to take our mistakes, if we will let Him, and turn them into blessings in our lives and the lives of others. Because God is PERFECT.

www.KUEST.org

WHAT YOU LEARNED ◯ DAY 5

Did you learn more about God's Love or God's Plan? Maybe you learned more about His Character or Truth. Place a checkmark in the box next to what you feel you learned about God. Then take a minute to write what you learned.

◯ **GOD'S LOVE**

◯ **GOD'S CHARACTER**

◯ **GOD'S TRUTH**

◯ **GOD'S PLAN**

Finish these final steps for today's journal. Checkmark each completed task.

● **HOW DO YOU PLAN TO MAKE THIS A PART OF YOUR EVERY DAY LIFE?**
[Write your answer in the appropriate **MY PLAN** Box in the back of this journal]

● **WHAT IS ONE POTENTIAL AREA OF WEAKNESS YOU WILL ASK THE HOLY SPIRIT TO HELP YOU MAKE STRONGER?**

[Stop now and ask the Holy Spirit for help in this area]

● **ENCOURAGE A FRIEND**
[Share empowering thoughts, ideas, words, and scriptures with your friends. Know what's going on in your friends lives. Make those things a matter of prayer. Find and share scriptures to encourage them.]

THE NAME OF THE FRIEND YOU ENCOURAGED:

THIS IS WHAT I DID: [circle all that you did]

called them   texted them   emailed them   talked to them   wrote a letter

26

MY PERSONAL NOTES

ME

WEEK #7
◯ DAY 1

Read the principle and the scriptures below. These are the ideas you want to have strong in your heart. Take your time and think about what you are reading. When you have finished this page, place a checkmark next to DAY 1.

PRINCIPLE

THE NATURE OF GOD IS GRACE

God IS Grace. Grace simply means that when we make a mistake, there is room for us to ask forgiveness and get it right. Without grace, we could never make it through life. The first time we ever made a mistake it would be over for us. But because God is full of Grace, we get a second chance. Because God is full of Grace we get to try again to make things right with those we've hurt, or to do what we know is right even when we blew it the first time. God can show us Grace because God loves us and wants to help us succeed.

SCRIPTURES
Growing in your knowledge of the Word.

☐ Ephesians 2:8 NLT God saved you by his grace when you believed. And you can't take credit for this; it is a gift from God.

☐ John 1:17 NKJV For the law was given through Moses, but grace and truth came through Jesus Christ.

☐ Romans 6:14 NLT Sin is no longer your master, for you no longer live under the requirements of the law. Instead, you live under the freedom of God's grace.

Place a check-mark next to the scripture you plan to memorize this week. Once you have recited it to a parent or leader, write the scripture in the appropriate box on your Memorized Word page.

28

© 2019 Current Family, Inc.

STRONGER HEART

For the next three days, you will read the lesson below. For each day you will mark the part of the lesson that stands out to you on that day. Each day requires you to use a different method. When you have completed marking the lesson for that day, checkmark the circle.

○ **DAY 2 |** <u>Underline</u>   ○ **DAY 3 |** (Circle)   ○ **DAY 4 | [Bracket]**

THE NATURE OF GOD IS <u>GRACE</u>.

What would it be like if the roads we drive on were the same exact width as our cars? What if the edge of the tires on our cars were right on the edge of the road and the edge of the road was a one-thousand-foot cliff on both sides? What if the sidewalk in your neighborhood was only six inches wide and on each side of the sidewalk was a great big lake of lava? If you made one mistake while driving on that road or made one bad step walking on that sidewalk, it would be really bad. Your car would fall off the edge of the cliff, or you would fall into a lake of lava. Thankfully, roads are made to be wide enough for our cars with room left over and our sidewalks are big enough to allow us to walk without worrying about falling off the edge. This is what GRACE looks like. Grace looks like the extra road outside the lines and the grass or dirt beside the sidewalk. Those things are there just in case we lose control or make a mistake. In the same way, God's Grace gives us room so that when we make mistakes we can get back on track with our lives. And God wants us to have grace with others, to be forgiving and to understand that sometimes people, including us, make mistakes and that grace will always be there to help us get back on track.

WHAT YOU LEARNED ○ DAY 5

Did you learn more about God's Love or God's Plan? Maybe you learned more about His Character or Truth. Place a checkmark in the box next to what you feel you learned about God. Then take a minute to write what you learned.

○ **GOD'S LOVE**

○ **GOD'S CHARACTER**

○ **GOD'S TRUTH**

○ **GOD'S PLAN**

Finish these final steps for today's journal. Checkmark each completed task.

○ **HOW DO YOU PLAN TO MAKE THIS A PART OF YOUR EVERY DAY LIFE?**

[Write your answer in the appropriate **MY PLAN** Box in the back of this journal]

○ **WHAT IS ONE POTENTIAL AREA OF WEAKNESS YOU WILL ASK THE HOLY SPIRIT TO HELP YOU MAKE STRONGER?**

[Stop now and ask the Holy Spirit for help in this area]

○ **ENCOURAGE A FRIEND**

[Share empowering thoughts, ideas, words, and scriptures with your friends. Know what's going on in your friends lives. Make those things a matter of prayer. Find and share scriptures to encourage them.]

THE NAME OF THE FRIEND YOU ENCOURAGED:

THIS IS WHAT I DID: [circle all that you did]

called them   texted them   emailed them   talked to them   wrote a letter

30

MY PERSONAL
NOTES

Read the principle and the scriptures below. These are the ideas you want to have strong in your heart. Take your time and think about what you are reading. When you have finished this page, place a checkmark next to DAY 1.

PRINCIPLE

THE PLAN OF GOD IS GENEROUS

God IS Generous. God has made more than enough fish, more than enough trees, more than enough sky. God has more than enough power and wisdom and love for everyone! God not only has more than enough, He has not only made more than enough, but He wants to share all of what He has so we can have more than enough too. God is generous. When He blesses us He does it in a way that is more than we could have expected. God goes above and beyond with loving us, helping us and making sure we have all we need!

SCRIPTURES

Growing in your knowledge of the Word.

☐ Psalms 145:9 NLT The LORD is good to everyone. He showers compassion on all his creation.

☐ Isaiah 32:8 NLT But generous people plan to do what is generous, and they stand firm in their generosity.

☐ James 1:5 NLT If you need wisdom, ask our generous God, and he will give it to you. He will not rebuke you for asking.

Place a check-mark next to the scripture you plan to memorize this week. Once you have recited it to a parent or leader, write the scripture in the appropriate box on your Memorized Word page.

◯ DAYS 2-4

STRONGER HEART

For the next three days, you will read the lesson below. For each day you will mark the part of the lesson that stands out to you on that day. Each day requires you to use a different method. When you have completed marking the lesson for that day, checkmark the circle.

◯DAY 2 | Underline   ◯DAY 3 | Circle   ◯DAY 4 | [Bracket]

THE NATURE OF GOD IS GENEROUS.

Have you ever gone to a birthday party at a friend's house where they served cake and ice cream? What if when they brought out the cake with candles and began to sing the birthday song it was only one little cupcake, and that's all. And what if when they opened the ice cream to serve it, there was only enough for one scoop. If there were 20 or 30 kids, would there be enough cake and ice cream? How disappointed would you be? Now what if you went to another party and they brought out the cake and it was three feet wide and 4 feet long? What if there was so much ice cream that you could fill a kiddie pool and dive into it? How excited would you be? The love that God has for us and the wisdom He can share with us is like the 3 foot cake and kiddie pool full of ice cream. It is more than enough and the really cool thing is that God wants us to have all the love and wisdom and confidence and joy we want! We can ask God for anything because He is a generous God. His nature is generous and God wants us to be generous as well. He wants us to be blessed so we can be a blessing to others. He wants us to have more than enough so we can give and help others as well. God wants us to be generous because God is generous.

www.KUEST.org

WHAT YOU LEARNED ○ DAY 5

Did you learn more about God's Love or God's Plan? Maybe you learned more about His Character or Truth. Place a checkmark in the box next to what you feel you learned about God. Then take a minute to write what you learned.

○ **GOD'S LOVE**

○ **GOD'S CHARACTER**

○ **GOD'S TRUTH**

○ **GOD'S PLAN**

Finish these final steps for today's journal. Checkmark each completed task.

● **HOW DO YOU PLAN TO MAKE THIS A PART OF YOUR EVERY DAY LIFE?**
[Write your answer in the appropriate **MY PLAN** Box in the back of this journal]

● **WHAT IS ONE POTENTIAL AREA OF WEAKNESS YOU WILL ASK THE HOLY SPIRIT TO HELP YOU MAKE STRONGER?**

[Stop now and ask the Holy Spirit for help in this area]

● **ENCOURAGE A FRIEND**
[Share empowering thoughts, ideas, words, and scriptures with your friends. Know what's going on in your friends lives. Make those things a matter of prayer. Find and share scriptures to encourage them.]

THE NAME OF THE FRIEND YOU ENCOURAGED:

THIS IS WHAT I DID: [circle all that you did]

called them   texted them   emailed them   talked to them   wrote a letter

34

MY PERSONAL NOTES

Read the principle and the scriptures below. These are the ideas you want to have strong in your heart. Take your time and think about what you are reading. When you have finished this page, place a checkmark next to DAY 1.

PRINCIPLE

THE PLAN OF GOD IS SACRIFICE

Sacrifice is giving up something of great value so that you can have something even better. Sometimes making a sacrifice is really hard because we really love what we have to give up. Sometimes sacrifice is hard because we don't really think the new thing will be better or more valuable. God sacrificed Jesus for us. He gave Jesus up so that He could give us the chance to be saved. Jesus sacrificed his life. He gave up His life so that He could make forgiveness possible for us. God saw the value of our lives and gave Jesus up for us.

SCRIPTURES

Growing in your knowledge of the Word.

☐ Matthew 22:37 NLT Jesus replied, "'You must love the LORD your God with all your heart, all your soul, and all your mind.'

☐ Proverbs 3:5 NLT Trust in the LORD with all your heart; do not depend on your own understanding.

☐ Luke 17:33 NLT If you cling to your life, you will lose it, and if you let your life go, you will save it.

Place a check-mark next to the scripture you plan to memorize this week. Once you have recited it to a parent or leader, write the scripture in the appropriate box on your Memorized Word page.

36

○ **DAYS 2-4**

STRONGER HEART

For the next three days, you will read the lesson below. For each day you will mark the part of the lesson that stands out to you on that day. Each day requires you to use a different method. When you have completed marking the lesson for that day, checkmark the circle.

○ DAY 2 | <u>Underline</u>   ○ DAY 3 | (Circle)   ○ DAY 4 | [Bracket]

<u>SACRIFICE</u> MAKES US STRONGER.

If you have ever handed a cashier some money so that you could have a toy or clothes or a new game, then you know what it means to sacrifice. Every time you decide to give your hard-earned dollars in order to get that newest song, or shoes or book, you are making a sacrifice. You are taking something that has value and trading it for something you believe has as much or even more value. And the more it takes to buy what you want, the greater the sacrifice is for you. In other words, spending two quarters that you found in a jar at home for a candy sucker is probably not that hard. Spending one-hundred dollars that you worked all summer to earn is going to be much harder. Think about what God sacrificed for us. His son, Jesus. Think about what Jesus sacrificed for us, His life! Now think about what you are sacrificing for God. Is what you are sacrificing for God like the two quarters, or like the hard-earned one-hundred dollars? God's plan was to give up the best He had so He could have us as His children. Are you giving up your best for God? Is watching TV more valuable than reading your Bible? Are sports more valuable than going to church? Making difficult sacrifices to please God and love others is always going to make you stronger.

37

www.KUEST.org

WHAT YOU LEARNED ○ DAY 5

Did you learn more about God's Love or God's Plan? Maybe you learned more about His Character or Truth. Place a checkmark in the box next to what you feel you learned about God. Then take a minute to write what you learned.

○ **GOD'S LOVE**

○ **GOD'S CHARACTER**

○ **GOD'S TRUTH**

○ **GOD'S PLAN**

Finish these final steps for today's journal. Checkmark each completed task.

○ **HOW DO YOU PLAN TO MAKE THIS A PART OF YOUR EVERY DAY LIFE?**
[Write your answer in the appropriate **MY PLAN** Box in the back of this journal]

○ **WHAT IS ONE POTENTIAL AREA OF WEAKNESS YOU WILL ASK THE HOLY SPIRIT TO HELP YOU MAKE STRONGER?**

[Stop now and ask the Holy Spirit for help in this area]

○ **ENCOURAGE A FRIEND**
[Share empowering thoughts, ideas, words, and scriptures with your friends. Know what's going on in your friends lives. Make those things a matter of prayer. Find and share scriptures to encourage them.]

THE NAME OF THE FRIEND YOU ENCOURAGED:

THIS IS WHAT I DID: [circle all that you did]

called them   texted them   emailed them   talked to them   wrote a letter

MY PERSONAL NOTES

Read the principle and the scriptures below. These are the ideas you want to have strong in your heart. Take your time and think about what you are reading. When you have finished this page, place a checkmark next to DAY 1.

PRINCIPLE

THE PLAN OF GOD IS RELATIONSHIP

Friends, family, teammates, coaches, parents, cousins, classmates; these are all examples of relationships we have in our lives. A relationship is simply how we connect with other people. We connect with our family differently than we connect with our friends. Our connection with our teachers is not the same as our connection with our classmates. But being connected with others is God's plan for this life. He has built us to have important and strong relationships. And the most important relationship is our connection to Jesus.

SCRIPTURES

Growing in your knowledge of the Word.

☐ Ephesians 6:3 NIV If you honor your father and mother, "things will go well for you, and you will have a long life on the earth."

☐ Ecclesiastes 4:9 NLT Two people are better off than one, for they can help each other succeed.

☐ Proverbs 27:17 NLT As iron sharpens iron, so a friend sharpens a friend.

Place a check-mark next to the scripture you plan to memorize this week. Once you have recited it to a parent or leader, write the scripture in the appropriate box on your Memorized Word page.

For the next three days, you will read the lesson below. For each day you will mark the part of the lesson that stands out to you on that day. Each day requires you to use a different method. When you have completed marking the lesson for that day, checkmark the circle.

◯DAY 2 | <u>Underline</u>   ◯DAY 3 | Ⓒircle   ◯DAY 4 | [Bracket]

<u>RELATIONSHIP</u> MAKES US STRONGER.

You hang out and play with your friends. You eat dinner with your family. Your coach helps you get better in the sport you play. Your classmates study school subjects and do projects with you. Your teachers at church help you grow in God's Word and faith. Every connection you have with the people around you is for a special purpose in your life. Relationships help us grow and stay strong; they help us have fun and enjoy life; they correct us and guide us and give us courage. Like Lego blocks, relationships come in many different shapes and sizes and colors, but they all connect in the same way. All of these connections create some really cool and special designs that we call our life. In fact, relationships are God's plan for how we live and enjoy life. And the greatest, most important relationship we have is our relationship, our connection, to Jesus. Jesus is like the big square Lego board that we use to build our creations on. He is what helps to hold our lives together. Every relationship we build should be built on our connection to Jesus. That's God's plan: strong connections with others that are built on a strong connection with Jesus. God wants us to have good, healthy relationships and those begin with our connection with Jesus.

Did you learn more about God's Love or God's Plan? Maybe you learned more about His Character or Truth. Place a checkmark in the box next to what you feel you learned about God. Then take a minute to write what you learned.

○ **GOD'S LOVE**

○ **GOD'S CHARACTER**

○ **GOD'S TRUTH**

○ **GOD'S PLAN**

Finish these final steps for today's journal. Checkmark each completed task.

● **HOW DO YOU PLAN TO MAKE THIS A PART OF YOUR EVERY DAY LIFE?**

[Write your answer in the appropriate **MY PLAN** Box in the back of this journal]

● **WHAT IS ONE POTENTIAL AREA OF WEAKNESS YOU WILL ASK THE HOLY SPIRIT TO HELP YOU MAKE STRONGER?**

[Stop now and ask the Holy Spirit for help in this area]

● **ENCOURAGE A FRIEND**

[Share empowering thoughts, ideas, words, and scriptures with your friends. Know what's going on in your friends lives. Make those things a matter of prayer. Find and share scriptures to encourage them.]

THE NAME OF THE FRIEND YOU ENCOURAGED:

THIS IS WHAT I DID: [circle all that you did]

called them   texted them   emailed them   talked to them   wrote a letter

MY PERSONAL NOTES

Read the principle and the scriptures below. These are the ideas you want to have strong in your heart. Take your time and think about what you are reading. When you have finished this page, place a checkmark next to DAY 1.

PRINCIPLE

THE PLAN OF GOD IS COMMUNITY

All the relationships you have with all the people around you, family, friends and so on, make up what is called your community. A community of people is simply people who have something in COMMON that UNIFIES them. They have a COMMon UNITY, or a COMM-UNITY. Our community of relationships is one of the biggest influences in our lives. It is one of the biggest reasons we become who we are. And God's plan for us is to have and enjoy a strong and healthy community of relationships.

SCRIPTURES

Growing in your knowledge of the Word.

☐ Proverbs 13:20 NLT Walk with the wise and become wise; associate with fools and get in trouble.

☐ Genesis 2:18 NLT Then the LORD God said, "It is not good for the man to be alone. I will make a helper who is just right for him."

☐ 1 Corinthians 1:10 NLT I appeal to you, dear brothers and sisters, by the authority of our Lord Jesus Christ, to live in harmony with each other. Let there be no divisions in the church. Rather, be of one mind, united in thought and purpose.

Place a check-mark next to the scripture you plan to memorize this week. Once you have recited it to a parent or leader, write the scripture in the appropriate box on your Memorized Word page.

44

○ DAYS 2-4

STRONGER HEART

For the next three days, you will read the lesson below. For each day you will mark the part of the lesson that stands out to you on that day. Each day requires you to use a different method. When you have completed marking the lesson for that day, checkmark the circle.

○ DAY 2 | <u>Underline</u>   ○ DAY 3 | (Circle)   ○ DAY 4 | [Bracket]

COMMUNITY MAKES US STRONGER.

God wants us to get together; especially with our faith friends. From the very beginning of time, God created us to have relationships with others. After God made Adam, He saw that Adam would need someone so that he would not be alone, so God made Eve. Adam and Eve had the first family and started the first community. God wants us to have good, meaningful, important and encouraging relationships; friendships that help us be our best. Being part of a healthy group of people (family and friends) means that we have all the answers and resources that we need to live a good life. Being part of a community of faith (church) means that we can grow stronger in our relationship with God and find purpose for our lives. Community is not only important for what we get from it, but also for what we give to it. Our role is to encourage others, to cheer them on, to dig in and help when they need help, to look out for each other and to love them with all our heart. This is why it is important to make the time your church - the community of believers - gets together an important part of your life. Family, friends and church are God's plan for helping us to live a healthy, exciting and fun life.

WHAT YOU LEARNED ○ DAY 5

Did you learn more about God's Love or God's Plan? Maybe you learned more about His Character or Truth. Place a checkmark in the box next to what you feel you learned about God. Then take a minute to write what you learned.

○ **GOD'S LOVE**

○ **GOD'S CHARACTER**

○ **GOD'S TRUTH**

○ **GOD'S PLAN**

Finish these final steps for today's journal. Checkmark each completed task.

● **HOW DO YOU PLAN TO MAKE THIS A PART OF YOUR EVERY DAY LIFE?**
[Write your answer in the appropriate **MY PLAN** Box in the back of this journal]

● **WHAT IS ONE POTENTIAL AREA OF WEAKNESS YOU WILL ASK THE HOLY SPIRIT TO HELP YOU MAKE STRONGER?**

[Stop now and ask the Holy Spirit for help in this area]

● **ENCOURAGE A FRIEND**
[Share empowering thoughts, ideas, words, and scriptures with your friends. Know what's going on in your friends lives. Make those things a matter of prayer. Find and share scriptures to encourage them.]

THE NAME OF THE FRIEND YOU ENCOURAGED:

THIS IS WHAT I DID: [circle all that you did]

called them   texted them   emailed them   talked to them   wrote a letter

46

MY PERSONAL
NOTES

Read the principle and the scriptures below. These are the ideas you want to have strong in your heart. Take your time and think about what you are reading. When you have finished this page, place a checkmark next to DAY 1.

PRINCIPLE

THE PLAN OF GOD IS PEACE & JOY

Anger, hatred, frustration, fear, depression, selfishness, lonliness; none of these are God's plan for us. In fact, God's plan for us is exactly the opposite of all these things. God wants us to experience a life that is filed with peace and joy. God has paid a great price, He has given His only Son Jesus, so that we could have peace and joy. Having peace means that we are at ease, with no fear about what may or may not happen. When we have joy, we are excited and find pleasure in what we have and what our future holds.

SCRIPTURES

Growing in your knowledge of the Word.

☐ Isaiah 26:3 NLT You will keep in perfect peace all who trust in you, all whose thoughts are fixed on you!

☐ Philippians 4:7 GWT Then God's peace, which goes beyond anything we can imagine, will guard your thoughts and emotions through Christ Jesus.

☐ Romans 15:13 NIV May the God of hope fill you with all joy and peace as you trust in him, so that you may overflow with hope by the power of the Holy Spirit.

Place a check-mark next to the scripture you plan to memorize this week. Once you have recited it to a parent or leader, write the scripture in the appropriate box on your Memorized Word page.

48

STRONGER HEART

For the next three days, you will read the lesson below. For each day you will mark the part of the lesson that stands out to you on that day. Each day requires you to use a different method. When you have completed marking the lesson for that day, checkmark the circle.

○ DAY 2 | <u>Underline</u>   ○ DAY 3 | (Circle)   ○ DAY 4 | [Bracket]

GOD'S PLAN IS PEACE & JOY

Someone accidentally ruins your favorite shirt and you get angry. Someone else says something mean to you and you say, "I hate you!" You hear a noise in the night and suddenly are very afraid. A friend asks if you will share some of your candy with them, and you selfishly say, "no." You are not able to paint the picture like you would like to and you become frustrated and begin to cry. Your friends all get to go a movie but you have to stay home and you feel alone and left out. Life is full of moments that want to cause us to get angry, frustrated, feel sad, be hateful, feel alone and even act selfishly. But God's plan for us is to live a life that is filled with peace and joy, where we share well with others and forgive quickly. He has paid a great price so that we can learn a new and better way of living every day. Through Jesus, He helps us to find peace when we feel like wrong has been done to us. His Word will help us overcome anger and fear by reminding us of the awesome Love of God. God does not create bad situations to make our life hard; instead, God is always at work in bad situations to help show us a way that we can make it out. God's plan is peace and joy. He wants us to sleep well at night in peace and to live life filled with Joy.

www.KUEST.org

WHAT YOU LEARNED ◯ DAY 5

Did you learn more about God's Love or God's Plan? Maybe you learned more about His Character or Truth. Place a checkmark in the box next to what you feel you learned about God. Then take a minute to write what you learned.

◯ **GOD'S LOVE**

◯ **GOD'S CHARACTER**

◯ **GOD'S TRUTH**

◯ **GOD'S PLAN**

Finish these final steps for today's journal. Checkmark each completed task.

◯ **HOW DO YOU PLAN TO MAKE THIS A PART OF YOUR EVERY DAY LIFE?**
[Write your answer in the appropriate **MY PLAN** Box in the back of this journal]

◯ **WHAT IS ONE POTENTIAL AREA OF WEAKNESS YOU WILL ASK THE HOLY SPIRIT TO HELP YOU MAKE STRONGER?**

[Stop now and ask the Holy Spirit for help in this area]

◯ **ENCOURAGE A FRIEND**
[Share empowering thoughts, ideas, words, and scriptures with your friends. Know what's going on in your friends lives. Make those things a matter of prayer. Find and share scriptures to encourage them.]

THE NAME OF THE FRIEND YOU ENCOURAGED:

THIS IS WHAT I DID: [circle all that you did]

called them   texted them   emailed them   talked to them   wrote a letter

50

MY PERSONAL
NOTES

Read the principle and the scriptures below. These are the ideas you want to have strong in your heart. Take your time and think about what you are reading. When you have finished this page, place a checkmark next to DAY 1.

PRINCIPLE

GOD BLESSES HIS CHILDREN

When we choose to believe in God, the Bible says we are His children. As God's children, we are loved by God. Like a great father, God loves His children very much. Because God loves His children, He blesses His children. He has made a way for His children to be taken care of in this life. For us, the blessings of God are all around us. We are blessed to have God in our lives. We are blessed to have His Word to live by. We are blessed in so many ways because we are His children. Every day we can be glad that God blesses His Children.

SCRIPTURES
Growing in your knowledge of the Word.

☐ Proverbs 10:22 NLT The blessing of the LORD makes a person rich, and he adds no sorrow with it.

☐ 2 Corinthians 9:8 NLT And God will generously provide all you need. Then you will always have everything you need and plenty left over to share with others.

☐ Deuteronomy 28:2 NIV All these blessings will come on you and accompany you if you obey the LORD your God:

Place a check-mark next to the scripture you plan to memorize this week. Once you have recited it to a parent or leader, write the scripture in the appropriate box on your Memorized Word page.

For the next three days, you will read the lesson below. For each day you will mark the part of the lesson that stands out to you on that day. Each day requires you to use a different method. When you have completed marking the lesson for that day, checkmark the circle.

○ DAY 2 | Underline   ○ DAY 3 | Circle   ○ DAY 4 | [Bracket]

WHAT DOES IT MEAN TO BE BLESSED?

Most of the time we think of a blessing as something that we receive, like a new bike or new clothes or a special trip with family or friends. But did you know that a blessing is much more than just stuff we might get? When we see the word "blessing" in the Bible, it means a lot more than gifts. It means a way of life. Blessing is not just about what we have, but how we live, our relationships, health in our bodies, peace in our minds and, most importantly, being at peace with God. Just because someone may have a bunch of toys or games or clothes or money does not necessarily mean they are blessed by God. Blessing only comes when we are in a relationship with God. In other words, blessing first begins in our heart. Our life is blessed first because God has accepted us as His own through our faith and believing in Him. Once we are in a relationship with Jesus, every part of our life becomes blessed. From there, we begin to see that life IS a blessing. We see friends as blessings. We see the food we have to eat as a huge blessing. We see the clothes we have and the toys we enjoy and all the things we love about life as true blessings! Loving God and being Loved by God is what it means to live the Blessed life - everything else is just extra!

WHAT YOU LEARNED ○ DAY 5

Did you learn more about God's Love or God's Plan? Maybe you learned more about His Character or Truth. Place a checkmark in the box next to what you feel you learned about God. Then take a minute to write what you learned.

○ **GOD'S LOVE**

○ **GOD'S CHARACTER**

○ **GOD'S TRUTH**

○ **GOD'S PLAN**

Finish these final steps for today's journal. Checkmark each completed task.

○ **HOW DO YOU PLAN TO MAKE THIS A PART OF YOUR EVERY DAY LIFE?**
[Write your answer in the appropriate **MY PLAN** Box in the back of this journal]

○ **WHAT IS ONE POTENTIAL AREA OF WEAKNESS YOU WILL ASK THE HOLY SPIRIT TO HELP YOU MAKE STRONGER?**

[Stop now and ask the Holy Spirit for help in this area]

○ **ENCOURAGE A FRIEND**
[Share empowering thoughts, ideas, words, and scriptures with your friends. Know what's going on in your friends lives. Make those things a matter of prayer. Find and share scriptures to encourage them.]

THE NAME OF THE FRIEND YOU ENCOURAGED:

THIS IS WHAT I DID: [circle all that you did]

called them   texted them   emailed them   talked to them   wrote a letter

MY PERSONAL
NOTES

WEEK #14
◯ DAY 1

Read the principle and the scriptures below. These are the ideas you want to have strong in your heart. Take your time and think about what you are reading. When you have finished this page, place a checkmark next to DAY 1.

PRINCIPLE

NOT A BLESSING IN DISGUISE

The Bible is very clear about what it means to be blessed and what it means to be cursed. There is no confusion in the Word of God about blessings and curses, good things and bad things in our lives and where they come from. For those who Love God and live their lives to please Him, we can live free from curses. When bad things happen to good people, they are not a blessing disguised as a curse. God does not make people sick. God does not punish His children with sickness or poverty. Curses are not blessings in disguise.

SCRIPTURES

Growing in your knowledge of the Word.

☐ Psalm 103:2 KJV Bless the LORD, O my soul, and forget not all his benefits:

☐ James 1:17 NLT Whatever is good and perfect comes down to us from God our Father, who created all the lights in the heavens. He never changes or casts a shifting shadow.

☐ Philippians 4:19 NIV And my God will meet all your needs according to the riches of his glory in Christ Jesus.

Place a check-mark next to the scripture you plan to memorize this week. Once you have recited it to a parent or leader, write the scripture in the appropriate box on your Memorized Word page.

56

STRONGER HEART

For the next three days, you will read the lesson below. For each day you will mark the part of the lesson that stands out to you on that day. Each day requires you to use a different method. When you have completed marking the lesson for that day, checkmark the circle.

○DAY 2 | <u>Underline</u>   ○DAY 3 | (Circle)   ○DAY 4 | [Bracket]

BAD STUFF IS NOT A BLESSING!

Someone knocks on your door and when you open the door you see Spiderman! WOW!! Spiderman is at your house! Not really, it's just your friend in a Spiderman costume coming over to spend the night and they wanted to surprise you. You laugh as they take off the mask and come in to start having fun. You and I both know that when they have that mask on they are not actually Spiderman. They are just dressing up like Spiderman. Putting that suit on does not give them the power to climb walls or swing from spider webs from building to building or to sense when trouble is around the corner. Even when they are dressed like Spiderman, they are just a normal, everyday friend who can't outrun your dog. In the same way, when bad things happen in our lives, they are not *Good Things* wearing a *Bad Things* costume. Bad things are bad and we should never treat them like good things. When we are sick we can pray and believe to get better. When someone hurts our feelings or treats us meanly we can pray and find a way to forgive them. Good may come from these bad moments, but the bad moments are not good. They may help us get stronger in our faith, but they are not good. The Devil's plan is bad stuff, God's plan is and always will be blessings.

www.KUEST.org

WHAT YOU LEARNED ○ DAY 5

Did you learn more about God's Love or God's Plan? Maybe you learned more about His Character or Truth. Place a checkmark in the box next to what you feel you learned about God. Then take a minute to write what you learned.

○ **GOD'S LOVE**

○ **GOD'S CHARACTER**

○ **GOD'S TRUTH**

○ **GOD'S PLAN**

Finish these final steps for today's journal. Checkmark each completed task.

● **HOW DO YOU PLAN TO MAKE THIS A PART OF YOUR EVERY DAY LIFE?**
[Write your answer in the appropriate **MY PLAN** Box in the back of this journal]

● **WHAT IS ONE POTENTIAL AREA OF WEAKNESS YOU WILL ASK THE HOLY SPIRIT TO HELP YOU MAKE STRONGER?**

[Stop now and ask the Holy Spirit for help in this area]

● **ENCOURAGE A FRIEND**
[Share empowering thoughts, ideas, words, and scriptures with your friends. Know what's going on in your friends lives. Make those things a matter of prayer. Find and share scriptures to encourage them.]

THE NAME OF THE FRIEND YOU ENCOURAGED:

THIS IS WHAT I DID: [circle all that you did]

called them   texted them   emailed them   talked to them   wrote a letter

MY PERSONAL
NOTES

Read the principle and the scriptures below. These are the ideas you want to have strong in your heart. Take your time and think about what you are reading. When you have finished this page, place a checkmark next to DAY 1.

PRINCIPLE

GOD WILL TAKE YOU THROUGH

Throughout the Bible there are stories about people who faced very tough times. Noah had to build a boat and save his family from a flood. Daniel had to face hungry lions. Shadrac, Meshac and Abednego were put into a fiery furnace. Paul was put in prison. The disciples were made fun of and hated. Jesus was beaten and crucified. In every one of those stories God made a way for them to make it out of those moments. No matter what you face in life, when you put your faith in God, He will help you make it through.

SCRIPTURES
Growing in your knowledge of the Word.

☐ Deuteronomy 31:6 NIV Be strong and courageous. Do not be afraid or terrified because of them, for the LORD your God goes with you; he will never leave you nor forsake you."

☐ Psalm 32:7 NLT For you are my hiding place; you protect me from trouble. You surround me with songs of victory.

☐ Psalm 34:17 NLT For the angel of the LORD is a guard; he surrounds and defends all who fear him.

Place a check-mark next to the scripture you plan to memorize this week. Once you have recited it to a parent or leader, write the scripture in the appropriate box on your Memorized Word page.

STRONGER HEART

For the next three days, you will read the lesson below. For each day you will mark the part of the lesson that stands out to you on that day. Each day requires you to use a different method. When you have completed marking the lesson for that day, checkmark the circle.

○ **DAY 2 | Underline**   ○ **DAY 3 | Circle**   ○ **DAY 4 | [Bracket]**

FINDING JOY IN TOUGH TIMES

One day, when my son Grant was about 6 years old, we were walking together through a corn-maze. We were laughing and having fun as we turned corner after corner and ran into a few dead-ends. Grant started to get tired, and it was getting hot, so we decided to leave the corn maze and find the rest of our family. The only problem was that we could not find our way out. It seemed like we were walking in circles and every option was the wrong direction. We finally ran into some other people who seemed like they knew where they were going and asked for help. They pointed us in the right direction and were soon out of the corn maze. Sometimes, this is how it is in life. We get stuck because of bad decisions. We find ourselves in a situation where there seems to be no way out and we feel like we are walking in circles. The good news is that we are never without the help of someone who knows everything and knows exactly what we need to do to escape the maze. Whether it is a sickness, help with schoolwork, an argument or a disagreement with a friend; no matter what we might be facing, if we will pray and ask God for help, He will lead us out. Jesus said that the Holy Spirit will lead us into all truth, that He would help us find a way through.

WHAT YOU LEARNED ○ DAY 5

Did you learn more about God's Love or God's Plan? Maybe you learned more about His Character or Truth. Place a checkmark in the box next to what you feel you learned about God. Then take a minute to write what you learned.

○ **GOD'S LOVE**

○ **GOD'S CHARACTER**

○ **GOD'S TRUTH**

○ **GOD'S PLAN**

Finish these final steps for today's journal. Checkmark each completed task.

○ **HOW DO YOU PLAN TO MAKE THIS A PART OF YOUR EVERY DAY LIFE?**
[Write your answer in the appropriate **MY PLAN** Box in the back of this journal]

○ **WHAT IS ONE POTENTIAL AREA OF WEAKNESS YOU WILL ASK THE HOLY SPIRIT TO HELP YOU MAKE STRONGER?**

[Stop now and ask the Holy Spirit for help in this area]

○ **ENCOURAGE A FRIEND**
[Share empowering thoughts, ideas, words, and scriptures with your friends. Know what's going on in your friends lives. Make those things a matter of prayer. Find and share scriptures to encourage them.]

THE NAME OF THE FRIEND YOU ENCOURAGED:

THIS IS WHAT I DID: [circle all that you did]

called them   texted them   emailed them   talked to them   wrote a letter

62

MY PERSONAL
NOTES

Read the principle and the scriptures below. These are the ideas you want to have strong in your heart. Take your time and think about what you are reading. When you have finished this page, place a checkmark next to DAY 1.

PRINCIPLE
THE JOY OF THE LORD IS OUR STRENGTH

Strength is what we use to carry a heavy load. Sometimes those loads are physical, like a suitcase or a large rock. Sometimes those loads are emotional, like receiving bad news or losing something valuable. Sometimes those loads are spiritual, like having to make tough choices or stand up for what you know is right. Whenever we need extra strength to carry a heavy load, we can trust that the Joy of knowing God Loves us will help us be stronger. It gives us the physical, emotional and spiritual endurance we need to carry the heavy load.

SCRIPTURES
Growing in your knowledge of the Word.

☐ James 1:2 NIV Consider it pure joy, my brothers and sisters, whenever you face trials of many kinds,

☐ Psalm 16:11 NIV You make known to me the path of life; you will fill me with joy in your presence, with eternal pleasures at your right hand.

☐ Nehemiah 8:10 NLT Don't be dejected and sad, for the joy of the LORD is your strength!"

Place a check-mark next to the scripture you plan to memorize this week. Once you have recited it to a parent or leader, write the scripture in the appropriate box on your Memorized Word page.

⭕ DAYS 2-4

STRONGER HEART

For the next three days, you will read the lesson below. For each day you will mark the part of the lesson that stands out to you on that day. Each day requires you to use a different method. When you have completed marking the lesson for that day, checkmark the circle.

⭕ **DAY 2 | <u>Underline</u>**   ⭕ **DAY 3 | (Circle)**   ⭕ **DAY 4 | [Bracket]**

STRENGTH TO ENDURE

Sometimes we have bad days that just don't go the way we want them to. Maybe your schoolwork is taking longer than expected and you are not able to get outside with friends. Maybe your game got rained out. Maybe you got hurt and had to spend the day on the couch. There are many things that can cause a day to go wrong and all of them can make us very upset. It can be a real bummer when we have big plans and something unexpected keeps us from those plans. When these things happen, we have a choice. We can either be upset and complain and get mad, or we can find a way to keep our joy even though it is tough. The great thing is that when life tosses us a lemon, the Holy Spirit will help us make some lemonade! Getting upset is likely not going to change the situation, but keeping your joy will definitely change your attitude. With God's help and with determination, we can stay in faith and find a way to keep our joy even though the moment is difficult. We do this by choosing to find the good no matter what comes our way. The injury means extra rest. The extra schoolwork is making us smarter. It might take work, but learning to keep your joy and a good attitude through tough times is well worth the effort.

WHAT YOU LEARNED ○ DAY 5

Did you learn more about God's Love or God's Plan? Maybe you learned more about His Character or Truth. Place a checkmark in the box next to what you feel you learned about God. Then take a minute to write what you learned.

○ **GOD'S LOVE**

○ **GOD'S CHARACTER**

○ **GOD'S TRUTH**

○ **GOD'S PLAN**

Finish these final steps for today's journal. Checkmark each completed task.

● **HOW DO YOU PLAN TO MAKE THIS A PART OF YOUR EVERY DAY LIFE?**
[Write your answer in the appropriate **MY PLAN** Box in the back of this journal]

● **WHAT IS ONE POTENTIAL AREA OF WEAKNESS YOU WILL ASK THE HOLY SPIRIT TO HELP YOU MAKE STRONGER?**

[Stop now and ask the Holy Spirit for help in this area]

● **ENCOURAGE A FRIEND**
[Share empowering thoughts, ideas, words, and scriptures with your friends. Know what's going on in your friends lives. Make those things a matter of prayer. Find and share scriptures to encourage them.]

THE NAME OF THE FRIEND YOU ENCOURAGED:

THIS IS WHAT I DID: [circle all that you did]

called them   texted them   emailed them   talked to them   wrote a letter

66

MY PERSONAL
NOTES

WEEK #17
○ DAY 1

Read the principle and the scriptures below. These are the ideas you want to have strong in your heart. Take your time and think about what you are reading. When you have finished this page, place a checkmark next to DAY 1.

PRINCIPLE
AN EXAMPLE IS A PATTERN

The Bible instructs us to be an example to everyone with our life: with our words, our actions, how we love, how we trust God, and by the moral values we choose. Did you know you have the choice to be a GOOD pattern, or a BAD pattern? You have the choice to be someone that others should imitate, and you also have the choice to be someone that others should avoid imitating. The truth is, because God is in you, YOU have the POWER to be a GOOD example that others can watch and imitate.

SCRIPTURES
Growing in your knowledge of the Word.

☐ 1 Timothy 4:12 NIV Don't let anyone look down on you because you are young, but set an example for the believers in speech, in conduct, in love, in faith and in purity.

☐ Titus 2:7 ESV Show yourself in all respects to be a model of good works,

☐ Romans 12:1-2 NIV Do not conform to the pattern of this world, but be transformed by the renewing of your mind. Then you will be able to test and approve what God's will is--his good, pleasing and perfect will.

Place a check-mark next to the scripture you plan to memorize this week. Once you have recited it to a parent or leader, write the scripture in the appropriate box on your Memorized Word page.

68

STRONGER HEART

For the next three days, you will read the lesson below. For each day you will mark the part of the lesson that stands out to you on that day. Each day requires you to use a different method. When you have completed marking the lesson for that day, checkmark the circle.

○DAY 2 | <u>Underline</u>   ○DAY 3 | (Circle)   ○DAY 4 | [Bracket]

AN EXAMPLE IS A PATTERN

Have you ever watched a Kids Baking Competition? Imagine, for a moment, that you were chosen to be a contestant. To prepare for the show, you were asked to bring the one recipe that you think would be THE GREATEST pattern from which you would make six dozen, delicious cupcakes. You find your grandmother's treasured recipe book, write the recipe of your favorite cupcakes, pack your bags, go to the airport, and after an exciting flight, arrive on the show with your recipe in hand! However, in the rush of it all, imagine you left some key ingredients out of the recipe! What if you left out baking soda? Your cupcakes would be flat instead of fluffy and yummy. What if you forgot to include butter or sugar? Who would want to eat a salty, pasty, dough ball without sugar!? Do you think you would have the award-winning, trophy-deserving cupcakes? Likely not. Just like a recipe is the perfect pattern for creating delicious cupcakes, When we pay attention to God's Word and choose to obey what it says, we are creating a pattern in our life that can be imitated. This kind of life pleases God, it keeps us protected, and it produces award-winning days and seasons in our life that are as sweet as....award-winning, Championship cupcakes, oozing with the best icing and toppings!

WHAT YOU LEARNED ○ DAY 5

Did you learn more about God's Love or God's Plan? Maybe you learned more about His Character or Truth. Place a checkmark in the box next to what you feel you learned about God. Then take a minute to write what you learned.

○ GOD'S LOVE

○ GOD'S CHARACTER

○ GOD'S TRUTH

○ GOD'S PLAN

Finish these final steps for today's journal. Checkmark each completed task.

○ HOW DO YOU PLAN TO MAKE THIS A PART OF YOUR EVERY DAY LIFE?
[Write your answer in the appropriate **MY PLAN** Box in the back of this journal]

○ WHAT IS ONE POTENTIAL AREA OF WEAKNESS YOU WILL ASK THE HOLY SPIRIT TO HELP YOU MAKE STRONGER?

[Stop now and ask the Holy Spirit for help in this area]

○ ENCOURAGE A FRIEND
[Share empowering thoughts, ideas, words, and scriptures with your friends. Know what's going on in your friends lives. Make those things a matter of prayer. Find and share scriptures to encourage them.]

THE NAME OF THE FRIEND YOU ENCOURAGED:

THIS IS WHAT I DID: [circle all that you did]

called them   texted them   emailed them   talked to them   wrote a letter

MY PERSONAL NOTES

Read the principle and the scriptures below. These are the ideas you want to have strong in your heart. Take your time and think about what you are reading. When you have finished this page, place a checkmark next to DAY 1.

PRINCIPLE

TAKING A RISK COMES BEFORE SUCCESS

When most people think of taking a risk, they think of things going wrong: like the possibility of loss or harm, sadness, or embarrassment. But there is another side to risk: the possibility of GAINING something, of INCREASING, of HAPPINESS and SUCCESS! In our lives, God doesn't want us to become stagnant, like a smelly pond. He desires for us to grow, have success, and fulfillment! Those things happen by taking risks, hearing and obeying. The Bible shows us the risk of obeying God is THE ONLY way to FULL SUCCESS!

SCRIPTURES

Growing in your knowledge of the Word.

☐ 2 Corinthians 5:7 NIV For we live by faith, not by sight.

☐ Hebrews 11:6 NLT And it is impossible to please God without faith. Anyone who wants to come to him must believe that God exists and that he rewards those who sincerely seek him.

☐ Deuteronomy 31:6 NLT So be strong and courageous! Do not be afraid and do not panic before them. For the LORD your God will personally go ahead of you. He will neither fail you nor abandon you."

Place a check-mark next to the scripture you plan to memorize this week. Once you have recited it to a parent or leader, write the scripture in the appropriate box on your Memorized Word page.

72

○ DAYS 2-4

STRONGER HEART

For the next three days, you will read the lesson below. For each day you will mark the part of the lesson that stands out to you on that day. Each day requires you to use a different method. When you have completed marking the lesson for that day, checkmark the circle.

○ DAY 2 | <u>Underline</u>   ○ DAY 3 | (Circle)   ○ DAY 4 | [Bracket]

TAKING A RISK COMES BEFORE SUCCESS

No risk, no reward. Every person that has accomplished anything amazing has reached success, and greatness, because they were willing to take a risk. What kind of risks should we take? God risks! We are to daringly do what God says we can do. The Bible says "ALL THINGS are possible for those who believe"… "I can do ALL THINGS through Christ who strengthens me,"….. "With God ALL THINGS are possible!" Those scriptures are more than just cool quotes for t-shirts. The are actually TRUE! People who believe these scriptures go on to see the reward of extraordinary things happening in their lives! Things like Noah building a huge boat to save humans and animals from the Great Flood; Moses lifting his staff and seeing an entire sea turn into two walls of water so millions of people could walk through; David, killing a smelly, loud-mouth giant who made fun of God; Esther, who, through a risky meeting with the King, saved the Jewish people from being destroyed. If God did it for them, He can do it for you. Living an extraordinary life requires taking the risk of faith. The devil will try to convince you to be fearful in your life, but if God is for you, who can be against you? There is NOTHING that is impossible for you, if you believe and are willing to take the risk of obeying God!

73

www.KUEST.org

WHAT YOU LEARNED ○ DAY 5

Did you learn more about God's Love or God's Plan? Maybe you learned more about His Character or Truth. Place a checkmark in the box next to what you feel you learned about God. Then take a minute to write what you learned.

○ **GOD'S LOVE**

○ **GOD'S CHARACTER**

○ **GOD'S TRUTH**

○ **GOD'S PLAN**

Finish these final steps for today's journal. Checkmark each completed task.

● **HOW DO YOU PLAN TO MAKE THIS A PART OF YOUR EVERY DAY LIFE?**
[Write your answer in the appropriate **MY PLAN** Box in the back of this journal]

● **WHAT IS ONE POTENTIAL AREA OF WEAKNESS YOU WILL ASK THE HOLY SPIRIT TO HELP YOU MAKE STRONGER?**

[Stop now and ask the Holy Spirit for help in this area]

● **ENCOURAGE A FRIEND**
[Share empowering thoughts, ideas, words, and scriptures with your friends. Know what's going on in your friends lives. Make those things a matter of prayer. Find and share scriptures to encourage them.]

THE NAME OF THE FRIEND YOU ENCOURAGED:

THIS IS WHAT I DID: [circle all that you did]

called them   texted them   emailed them   talked to them   wrote a letter

MY PERSONAL NOTES

Read the principle and the scriptures below. These are the ideas you want to have strong in your heart. Take your time and think about what you are reading. When you have finished this page, place a checkmark next to DAY 1.

PRINCIPLE
LISTEN TO YOUR CONSCIENCE

Your conscience is powerful. It is a sense of right and wrong, and the feeling that you should do what is right. God gave you a conscience as a very helpful tool. When you listen to and follow your conscience, you are more likely to do what is right, keeping you from harm, guilt, and consequences. Because your conscience is influenced by the Spirit of God, you have the power to do what is right EVERY TIME. You can choose to FOLLOW your conscience, or ignore it. God's Spirit gives you the power to make the right choice.

SCRIPTURES
Growing in your knowledge of the Word.

☐ Romans 8:14 NLT For all who are led by the Spirit of God are children of God.

☐ Romans 8:16 BLB The Spirit Himself bears witness with our spirit that we are children of God,

☐ Proverbs 20:27 KJV The spirit of man is the candle of the LORD, searching all the inward parts of the belly.

Place a check-mark next to the scripture you plan to memorize this week. Once you have recited it to a parent or leader, write the scripture in the appropriate box on your Memorized Word page.

76

STRONGER HEART

For the next three days, you will read the lesson below. For each day you will mark the part of the lesson that stands out to you on that day. Each day requires you to use a different method. When you have completed marking the lesson for that day, checkmark the circle.

○ **DAY 2 | <u>Underline</u>**   ○ **DAY 3 | (Circle)**   ○ **DAY 4 | [Bracket]**

LISTEN TO YOUR CONSCIENCE

Have you ever used a walkie-talkie while camping or hiking with friends? If you've ever been lost from your group, having a walkie-talkie can be an absolute lifesaver. On the right frequency, it can enable you to communicate with a trusted leader who can give you instruction, encouragement, warning, and direction – and lead you on the quickest path back to your safe campsite. You have built-in equipment very similar to this on the inside of you. It's called your spirit. Sometimes we refer to this communication mechanism as our conscience. God created your conscience to be a way for Truth and Wisdom to be downloaded to you. All of us know what it feels like to have our conscience speak to us when trying to make a decision between right and wrong. Whether it's a dishonest answer, completely rebelling against our parent's request, or ignoring instruction from Scripture, we understand that our conscience is always warning us about wrong decisions and trying to point us to what is right. God will never force you to listen to your conscience, but when you choose to listen, it is always to your advantage. Listening will keep you safe and lead you to God's best.

WHAT YOU LEARNED ○DAY 5

Did you learn more about God's Love or God's Plan? Maybe you learned more about His Character or Truth. Place a checkmark in the box next to what you feel you learned about God. Then take a minute to write what you learned.

○ **GOD'S LOVE**

○ **GOD'S CHARACTER**

○ **GOD'S TRUTH**

○ **GOD'S PLAN**

Finish these final steps for today's journal. Checkmark each completed task.

○ **HOW DO YOU PLAN TO MAKE THIS A PART OF YOUR EVERY DAY LIFE?**
[Write your answer in the appropriate **MY PLAN** Box in the back of this journal]

○ **WHAT IS ONE POTENTIAL AREA OF WEAKNESS YOU WILL ASK THE HOLY SPIRIT TO HELP YOU MAKE STRONGER?**

[Stop now and ask the Holy Spirit for help in this area]

○ **ENCOURAGE A FRIEND**
[Share empowering thoughts, ideas, words, and scriptures with your friends. Know what's going on in your friends lives. Make those things a matter of prayer. Find and share scriptures to encourage them.]

THE NAME OF THE FRIEND YOU ENCOURAGED:

THIS IS WHAT I DID: [circle all that you did]

called them   texted them   emailed them   talked to them   wrote a letter

MY PERSONAL NOTES

Read the principle and the scriptures below. These are the ideas you want to have strong in your heart. Take your time and think about what you are reading. When you have finished this page, place a checkmark next to DAY 1.

PRINCIPLE
INFLUENCE IS THE POWER TO CHANGE

INFLUENCE is the power to change or affect someone or something. You are being influenced by others' opinions, actions and words every day. Your parents, teachers, coaches, friends, even TV shows, and songs influence the way you think. They are forming parts of who you are. Whether you realize it or not, YOU are actually influencing people every day by your conversations and actions. YOU are influencing your family, friends, and those who are watching you.

SCRIPTURES
Growing in your knowledge of the Word.

- [ ] Colossians 4:5 NIV Be wise in the way you act toward outsiders; make the most of every opportunity.

- [ ] Matthew 5:16 NLT In the same way, let your good deeds shine out for all to see, so that everyone will praise your heavenly Father.

- [ ] Colossians 4:6 NLT Let your conversation be gracious and attractive so that you will have the right response for everyone.

Place a check-mark next to the scripture you plan to memorize this week. Once you have recited it to a parent or leader, write the scripture in the appropriate box on your Memorized Word page.

STRONGER
HEART

For the next three days, you will read the lesson below. For each day you will mark the part of the lesson that stands out to you on that day. Each day requires you to use a different method. When you have completed marking the lesson for that day, checkmark the circle.

○DAY 2 | <u>Underline</u>   ○DAY 3 | (Circle)   ○DAY 4 | [Bracket]

INFLUENCE IS THE POWER TO CHANGE

Imagine the perfect, summer day planned with one of your besties – a swim-day at the neighborhood pool! So, you jump onto your bikes with your swimsuits and backpacks and head to the street where you will pedal up a major incline, then descend down the other side, at full speed, with your legs stretched out and your toes feeling the breeze! Then unexpectedly, your front tire hits a rock, you lose control of the bike, and take a nasty dive. Your skin skids across the pavement, then 3, 2, 1, you are in severe pain from the road rash that covers your arms and legs. Instead of the enjoying the pool, you pick up your bike, and limp home for bandages and an ice pack. How did the perfect day turn into misery? That stinking rock. Your bike was INFLUENCED out of control when that rock CHANGED the direction of your tire and AFFECTED your entire day. This is an example of the power of INFLUENCE. It can cause damage or bring good. You INFLUENCE others with good words or harmful words. You INFLUENCE the environment of your home with your GOOD ATTITUDE, or BAD ATTITUDE. YOUR INFLUENCE MATTERS, so live every day like your words, your actions, your choices, and your attitudes matter, because they do!

WHAT YOU LEARNED ◯DAY 5

Did you learn more about God's Love or God's Plan? Maybe you learned more about His Character or Truth. Place a checkmark in the box next to what you feel you learned about God. Then take a minute to write what you learned.

◯ **GOD'S LOVE**

◯ **GOD'S CHARACTER**

◯ **GOD'S TRUTH**

◯ **GOD'S PLAN**

Finish these final steps for today's journal. Checkmark each completed task.

◯ **HOW DO YOU PLAN TO MAKE THIS A PART OF YOUR EVERY DAY LIFE?**
[Write your answer in the appropriate **MY PLAN** Box in the back of this journal]

◯ **WHAT IS ONE POTENTIAL AREA OF WEAKNESS YOU WILL ASK THE HOLY SPIRIT TO HELP YOU MAKE STRONGER?**

[Stop now and ask the Holy Spirit for help in this area]

◯ **ENCOURAGE A FRIEND**
[Share empowering thoughts, ideas, words, and scriptures with your friends. Know what's going on in your friends lives. Make those things a matter of prayer. Find and share scriptures to encourage them.]

THE NAME OF THE FRIEND YOU ENCOURAGED:

THIS IS WHAT I DID: [circle all that you did]

called them   texted them   emailed them   talked to them   wrote a letter

MY PERSONAL NOTES

Read the principle and the scriptures below. These are the ideas you want to have strong in your heart. Take your time and think about what you are reading. When you have finished this page, place a checkmark next to DAY 1.

PRINCIPLE

GOD IN US

IN indicates a LOCATION. Like, the popsicle is IN the freezer (not OUT of it). God is IN us. His LOCATION is IN us (not outside of us). IN also means to INCORPORATE. Like, I'm mixing IN the eggs to the brownie batter. (Once it is mixed IN, it's impossible to separate out). God is IN us. His Spirit INCORPORATES with us, and changes us from darkness to light, from death to life! We are spiritually alive because God is IN us!

SCRIPTURES
Growing in your knowledge of the Word.

☐ Romans 8:11 NLT The Spirit of God, who raised Jesus from the dead, lives in you. And just as God raised Christ Jesus from the dead, he will give life to your mortal bodies by this same Spirit living within you.

☐ 2 Corinthians 5:17 NLT This means that anyone who belongs to Christ has become a new person. The old life is gone; a new life has begun!

☐ Ephesians 3:17 NLT Then Christ will make his home in your hearts as you trust in him. Your roots will grow down into God's love and keep you strong.

Place a check-mark next to the scripture you plan to memorize this week. Once you have recited it to a parent or leader, write the scripture in the appropriate box on your Memorized Word page.

84

⭘ DAYS 2-4

For the next three days, you will read the lesson below. For each day you will mark the part of the lesson that stands out to you on that day. Each day requires you to use a different method. When you have completed marking the lesson for that day, checkmark the circle.

⭘DAY 2 | <u>Underline</u>   ⭘DAY 3 | (Circle)   ⭘DAY 4 | [Bracket]

GOD <u>IN</u> US

When we invite Christ to come into our life, HE makes HIS HOME in our heart (not the physical one, but the spiritual one). His Spirit actually comes to live inside of us and transforms us from death to LIFE! God loves you so much that He didn't want to be a far-away God. No, He wanted to make Himself available to you ALL THE TIME! He wanted to experience every second and every piece of life with you. Wake up every morning – He's there. Not just in heaven, but in your same space, as close as your breath! He is with you constantly – to let you know you are loved, so you wouldn't ever have to be afraid or lonely, so you wouldn't ever have to walk into any situation without Him RIGHT WITH YOU! That's why He made His home in YOUR HEART. You asked Jesus to come into your life, and, BOOM - He MOVED IN! AND, when He moved in, all of His awesomeness came with Him! He freely gives you ALL the power you need, the understanding you need, the help you need, the joy you need, the peace you need. It's like having a water fountain on the inside of you on the hottest of days! It's like having the wisest person in the Universe with you for every decision. He is IN you!

www.KUEST.org

WHAT YOU LEARNED ◯ DAY 5

Did you learn more about God's Love or God's Plan? Maybe you learned more about His Character or Truth. Place a checkmark in the box next to what you feel you learned about God. Then take a minute to write what you learned.

◯ **GOD'S LOVE**

◯ **GOD'S CHARACTER**

◯ **GOD'S TRUTH**

◯ **GOD'S PLAN**

Finish these final steps for today's journal. Checkmark each completed task.

◯ **HOW DO YOU PLAN TO MAKE THIS A PART OF YOUR EVERY DAY LIFE?**
[Write your answer in the appropriate **MY PLAN** Box in the back of this journal]

◯ **WHAT IS ONE POTENTIAL AREA OF WEAKNESS YOU WILL ASK THE HOLY SPIRIT TO HELP YOU MAKE STRONGER?**

[Stop now and ask the Holy Spirit for help in this area]

◯ **ENCOURAGE A FRIEND**
[Share empowering thoughts, ideas, words, and scriptures with your friends. Know what's going on in your friends lives. Make those things a matter of prayer. Find and share scriptures to encourage them.]

THE NAME OF THE FRIEND YOU ENCOURAGED:

THIS IS WHAT I DID: [circle all that you did]

called them   texted them   emailed them   talked to them   wrote a letter

MY PERSONAL NOTES

Read the principle and the scriptures below. These are the ideas you want to have strong in your heart. Take your time and think about what you are reading. When you have finished this page, place a checkmark next to DAY 1.

PRINCIPLE
FOLLOWING THE HOLY SPIRIT

If you had to write instructions for following a the leader, you might say: Let the leader go first. Go after them. Pay attention to the leader. Copy what they do. Stay with the leader. Allow them to tell you what to do. Do you know this is how you should FOLLOW The Holy Spirit? God sent Him to teach us ALL things, and to LEAD us into God's Plan! He knows EVERYTHING and is the Best Leader to follow!

SCRIPTURES
Growing in your knowledge of the Word.

☐ John 14:17 NLT He is the Holy Spirit, who leads into all truth. The world cannot receive him, because it isn't looking for him and doesn't recognize him. But you know him, because he lives with you now and later will be in you.

☐ John 14:26 NLT But when the Father sends the Advocate as my representative--that is, the Holy Spirit--he will teach you everything and will remind you of everything I have told you.

☐ John 16:13 NLT When the Spirit of truth comes, he will guide you into all truth. He will not speak on his own but will tell you what he has heard. He will tell you about the future.

Place a check-mark next to the scripture you plan to memorize this week. Once you have recited it to a parent or leader, write the scripture in the appropriate box on your Memorized Word page.

88

For the next three days, you will read the lesson below. For each day you will mark the part of the lesson that stands out to you on that day. Each day requires you to use a different method. When you have completed marking the lesson for that day, checkmark the circle.

○ **DAY 2 | Underline**   ○ **DAY 3 | Circle**   ○ **DAY 4 | [Bracket]**

FOLLOWING THE HOLY SPIRIT

Cedar Point is listed as one of the best amusement parks in the world! Just imagine that you won a birthday party at Cedar Point with the exclusive VIP Gold Tour experience! This fun package entitles you to your very own, personal, VIP Tour Guide! Your VIP Tour Guide is at your service, and never leaves you the entire day! He makes reservations at your FAVORITE park restaurant so you don't have to wait in line for food! He walks you past the lines to a FRONT ROW seat for every show you want to see. AND, the best thing? The VIP Tour Guide will escort you to WHATEVER ride you want, taking you up the exit side - so you hop on, and never wait in line at all for any ride in the park! Did you know that God designed a VIP Tour Guide for your entire life? The Holy Spirit. He is with you every moment and His Role is to help you, to teach you what you need to know, and remind you of everything (keep that in mind during your next exam!). He even shows us our future. He helps you get to all the GOOD things God has prepared for you, to help you live a life "far more than you could ever imagine or guess or request in your wildest dreams!" (Eph 3:20).

WHAT YOU LEARNED ○ DAY 5

Did you learn more about God's Love or God's Plan? Maybe you learned more about His Character or Truth. Place a checkmark in the box next to what you feel you learned about God. Then take a minute to write what you learned.

- ○ **GOD'S LOVE**

- ○ **GOD'S CHARACTER**

- ○ **GOD'S TRUTH**

- ○ **GOD'S PLAN**

Finish these final steps for today's journal. Checkmark each completed task.

○ **HOW DO YOU PLAN TO MAKE THIS A PART OF YOUR EVERY DAY LIFE?**
[Write your answer in the appropriate **MY PLAN** Box in the back of this journal]

○ **WHAT IS ONE POTENTIAL AREA OF WEAKNESS YOU WILL ASK THE HOLY SPIRIT TO HELP YOU MAKE STRONGER?**

[Stop now and ask the Holy Spirit for help in this area]

○ **ENCOURAGE A FRIEND**
[Share empowering thoughts, ideas, words, and scriptures with your friends. Know what's going on in your friends lives. Make those things a matter of prayer. Find and share scriptures to encourage them.]

THE NAME OF THE FRIEND YOU ENCOURAGED:

THIS IS WHAT I DID: [circle all that you did]

called them   texted them   emailed them   talked to them   wrote a letter

MY PERSONAL NOTES

WEEK #23
◯ DAY 1

Read the principle and the scriptures below. These are the ideas you want to have strong in your heart. Take your time and think about what you are reading. When you have finished this page, place a checkmark next to DAY 1.

PRINCIPLE
I PLAY AN IMPORTANT PART

To Belong means to be a part, or a function of a person or thing. You belong to a certain family, possibly a certain school, choir or sports team. YOU also belong to The Body of Christ. Wherever you live, God has designed you to BELONG (to be a part or function of) a CHURCH FAMILY. You have a unique role, using your gifts and talents to help your church express God's love to people who need Him!

SCRIPTURES
Growing in your knowledge of the Word.

☐ 1 Corinthians 12:27 NIV Now you are the body of Christ, and each one of you is a part of it.

☐ Romans 12:4,5 NLT Just as our bodies have many parts and each part has a special function, so it is with Christ's body. We are many parts of one body, and we all belong to each other.

☐ Ephesians 4:11 NLT Now these are the gifts Christ gave to the church: the apostles, the prophets, the evangelists, and the pastors and teachers.

Place a check-mark next to the scripture you plan to memorize this week. Once you have recited it to a parent or leader, write the scripture in the appropriate box on your Memorized Word page.

92

For the next three days, you will read the lesson below. For each day you will mark the part of the lesson that stands out to you on that day. Each day requires you to use a different method. When you have completed marking the lesson for that day, checkmark the circle.

◯DAY 2 | <u>Underline</u>   ◯DAY 3 | Circle   ◯DAY 4 | [Bracket]

I PLAY AN IMPORTANT PART

Every part of your body is essential and performs an important function. Your eyes, heart, kidney, and pinky are all important. Every one of us is like a body part. The gifts God has placed in us are unique and are to be used in our lives personally and within a local church. In your physical body, some parts are seen (like your nose), and some are not (like your lungs). They are BOTH extremely valuable. In the church, some people's gifts may be seen regularly (like a greeter in the lobby), and some may rarely be seen (like an assistant in the office). They are BOTH extremely valuable. Whatever your gifts and personality are, YOU are an ESSENTIAL part of the Body of Christ, and ESSENTIAL to your church family. Are you using your gifts and talents to serve? If you are gifted as an actor, dancer, vacuum operator, painter, or if you like to organize, use those skills in the church! By everyone KNOWING they BELONG and ACTING like they BELONG, the church body is strong and healthy and can connect more people to God's love, and a new life in Christ! You have GIFTS and TALENTS that God has placed in you to use for the benefit of others!

WHAT YOU LEARNED ⦾ DAY 5

Did you learn more about God's Love or God's Plan? Maybe you learned more about His Character or Truth. Place a checkmark in the box next to what you feel you learned about God. Then take a minute to write what you learned.

⦾ **GOD'S LOVE**

⦾ **GOD'S CHARACTER**

⦾ **GOD'S TRUTH**

⦾ **GOD'S PLAN**

Finish these final steps for today's journal. Checkmark each completed task.

⦾ **HOW DO YOU PLAN TO MAKE THIS A PART OF YOUR EVERY DAY LIFE?**
[Write your answer in the appropriate **MY PLAN** Box in the back of this journal]

⦾ **WHAT IS ONE POTENTIAL AREA OF WEAKNESS YOU WILL ASK THE HOLY SPIRIT TO HELP YOU MAKE STRONGER?**

[Stop now and ask the Holy Spirit for help in this area]

⦾ **ENCOURAGE A FRIEND**
[Share empowering thoughts, ideas, words, and scriptures with your friends. Know what's going on in your friends lives. Make those things a matter of prayer. Find and share scriptures to encourage them.]

THE NAME OF THE FRIEND YOU ENCOURAGED:

THIS IS WHAT I DID: [circle all that you did]

called them   texted them   emailed them   talked to them   wrote a letter

MY PERSONAL
NOTES

WEEK #24
○ DAY 1

Read the principle and the scriptures below. These are the ideas you want to have strong in your heart. Take your time and think about what you are reading. When you have finished this page, place a checkmark next to DAY 1.

PRINCIPLE
PRACTICE, PRACTICE, PRACTICE!

Practice is the act of doing something again and again in order to improve. Whether it's math, soccer kicks, landing a back handspring, expanding your vocal range, making others feel welcome, cleaning your room, or responding the first time when your parents call, you can make the choice to PRACTICE. Practice takes a decision of your will and a lot of space on your calendar. The more you practice something the better you will become.

SCRIPTURES
Growing in your knowledge of the Word.

- ☐ Timothy 2:15 NLT Work hard so you can present yourself to God and receive his approval. Be a good worker, one who does not need to be ashamed and who correctly explains the word of truth.

- ☐ Colossians 3:23 NLT Work willingly at whatever you do, as though you were working for the Lord rather than for people.

- ☐ Titus 2:7 ISV Always set an example for others by doing good actions. Teach with integrity and dignity.

Place a check-mark next to the scripture you plan to memorize this week. Once you have recited it to a parent or leader, write the scripture in the appropriate box on your Memorized Word page.

96

STRONGER HEART

For the next three days, you will read the lesson below. For each day you will mark the part of the lesson that stands out to you on that day. Each day requires you to use a different method. When you have completed marking the lesson for that day, checkmark the circle.

○DAY 2 | <u>Underline</u>   ○DAY 3 | Ⓒircle   ○DAY 4 | [Bracket]

PRACTICE, PRACTICE, PRACTICE!

If you have ever been a part of a sports team, you are well aware that to perform well, it takes practice! Drill after drill, the same play over and over. Have you ever enjoyed watching a great musical? Great performances do not just magically happen – they are a result of saying the same lines over and over, with hours of rehearsals. There are two main parts to practicing – the first part is your DECISION to practice. You CHOOSE to attend a practice, or to make yourself practice at home. Your WILL is involved. You say, "I AM GOING TO PRACTICE!" The second part is your ACTION to practice. It's more than just deciding and saying it, you go the next step to actually DO the practice! Do you know that it is God's desire that you PRACTICE using your gifts and talents so that you can become skillful? He has created you to use what you have on the inside, and get really GOOD at using those gifts. God gave you gifts so that you can use them, not just for yourself but to influence others for God. You are to become GOOD at using your gifts for the GOOD of OTHERS.

www.KUEST.org

WHAT YOU LEARNED ○ DAY 5

Did you learn more about God's Love or God's Plan? Maybe you learned more about His Character or Truth. Place a checkmark in the box next to what you feel you learned about God. Then take a minute to write what you learned.

○ **GOD'S LOVE**

○ **GOD'S CHARACTER**

○ **GOD'S TRUTH**

○ **GOD'S PLAN**

Finish these final steps for today's journal. Checkmark each completed task.

● **HOW DO YOU PLAN TO MAKE THIS A PART OF YOUR EVERY DAY LIFE?**
[Write your answer in the appropriate **MY PLAN** Box in the back of this journal]

● **WHAT IS ONE POTENTIAL AREA OF WEAKNESS YOU WILL ASK THE HOLY SPIRIT TO HELP YOU MAKE STRONGER?**

[Stop now and ask the Holy Spirit for help in this area]

● **ENCOURAGE A FRIEND**
[Share empowering thoughts, ideas, words, and scriptures with your friends. Know what's going on in your friends lives. Make those things a matter of prayer. Find and share scriptures to encourage them.]

THE NAME OF THE FRIEND YOU ENCOURAGED:

THIS IS WHAT I DID: [circle all that you did]

called them   texted them   emailed them   talked to them   wrote a letter

MY PERSONAL
NOTES

MEMORIZED WORD

Writing helps you remember. In your weekly entry, you placed a check mark next to the scripture you wanted to memorize. Take a moment and write that entire scripture in the corresponding week's box below. You can refer back to these pages in the weeks to come as part of your memorization process.

WEEK 1

WEEK 2

WEEK 3

WEEK 4

WEEK 5

WEEK 6

WEEK 7

WEEK 8

WEEK 9

WEEK 10

WEEK 11

WEEK 12

WEEK 13

WEEK 14

www.KUEST.org

WEEK 15

WEEK 16

WEEK 17

WEEK 18

WEEK 19

WEEK 20

WEEK 21

WEEK 22

WEEK 23

WEEK 24

MY PLAN

What is your plan for growth? Every week you are learning more about growing stronger in maturity and engagement. The boxes below correspond with the lessons for each week. Write in what you plan to do to grow stronger from what you have learned. When you have completed this journal, you will have an action plan for growth.

WEEK 1

WEEK 2

WEEK 3

WEEK 4

WEEK 5

WEEK 6

WEEK 7

WEEK 8

WEEK 9

WEEK 10

WEEK 11

WEEK 12

WEEK 13

WEEK 14

WEEK 15

WEEK 16

WEEK 17

WEEK 18

WEEK 19

WEEK 20

WEEK 21

WEEK 22

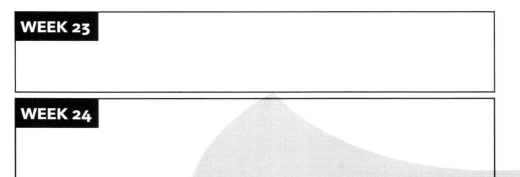

WEEK 23

WEEK 24

WELL DONE! You have finished your journal. You have grown in spiritual maturity and engagement. You are a stronger ME! We hope that these 24 weeks have given you greater confidence, knowledge, wisdom and courage. We believe that God has a great plan for your life. Please accept our prayers as we believe with you for a strong future!

"Father, we ask that you would continue to lead our friend by your Holy Spirit. We are thankful that they have completed this course and that they have opened their heart to You in a greater way. Help them to have clarity and strength to accomplish all you have for them. We are grateful to have offered this resource for them and now ask Your guidance, grace and peace upon their lives. In Jesus name, AMEN!"

Made in the USA
Middletown, DE
07 July 2021